MW00988856

OCD

Freedom for the
Obsessive-Compulsive

Resources for Changing Lives

A Ministry of
THE CHRISTIAN COUNSELING AND
EDUCATIONAL FOUNDATION
Glenside, Pennsylvania

RCL Ministry Booklets
Susan Lutz, Series Editor

OCD

Freedom for the Obsessive-Compulsive

Michael R. Emlet

P&R PUBLISHING
P.O. BOX 817 • PHILLIPSBURG • NEW JERSEY 08865-0817

© 2004 by Michael R. Emlet

Printed in the United States of America

Library of Congress Cataloging-in-Publication Data

Emlet, Michael R.
    OCD : freedom for the obsessive-compulsive / Michael R. Emlet.
        p. cm. — (Resources for changing lives)
    Includes bibliographical references.
    ISBN 10: 0-87552-698-5
    ISBN 13: 978-0-87552-698-0
    1. Obsessive-compulsive disorder—Popular works. 2. Ob-. sessive-compulsive disorder—Religious aspects—Christianity
I. Title. II. Series.

RC533.E456 2004
616.85'227—dc22   2004044153

Have you ever had a thought that was difficult to push from your mind? Have you ever gone to bed and asked yourself, "Did I lock the front door?" You're 99.9 percent sure that you did, but that last shred of doubt causes you to go downstairs and check, just to be sure. You find that, indeed, you did lock the door, so you trudge back to bed and quickly fall asleep, forgetting the incident. No problem!

This is a common and normal experience. But have you or anyone you know struggled in the following ways?

- After checking the door once, you lie in bed and wonder, "Did I absolutely make certain that the door was locked?" You fight the building anxiety, but eventually succumb to a cycle of checking and rechecking that continues until you fall asleep in sheer exhaustion at three a.m.
- You worry that your floors and household surfaces are not clean enough to prevent

contaminating your children. So, although you know your fear is irrational, you spend hours each day cleaning your house with Clorox.

- You stop driving for fear that you may hit and kill someone (although your driving record and skills are impeccable).
- You stop going to church because of an overwhelming fear that you will yell something blasphemous during the sermon.
- You feel unable to throw away the magazines and newspapers accumulating around the house. In fact, you can't bring yourself to throw out any piece of paper.

While these problems may seem extreme, as many as three percent of the United States population struggle in this manner to some degree. What causes this behavior? Is this primarily a spiritual or sin issue? Or is it principally a body issue in which a particular portion of brain circuitry fires in an endless loop, compelling you to carry out certain behaviors? These questions must be answered if we are to minister wisely and compassionately to those who struggle in this way.

This booklet will describe the experience

of what has been named Obsessive Compulsive Disorder, hereafter OCD. (I use this term for the sake of simplicity, though I disagree with the inference that OCD has a purely biological cause, as the word "disorder" might imply. That assumption ignores the spiritual aspect of our personhood.) I will discuss its possible causes, and suggest a biblical approach that does justice to the person as body and soul. Hopefully, you will gain greater clarity about how to approach your own (or another's) struggle with OCD.

What Is OCD?

The essential features of OCD include recurrent obsessions and/or compulsions that are severe enough to be time-consuming or to cause marked distress or significant impairment in a person's daily routine.[1]

Obsessions are "persistent ideas, thoughts, impulses, or images that are experienced as intrusive and inappropriate and cause marked anxiety or distress."[2] These ideas, thoughts, impulses, or images are not simply excessive worries about actual problems (with things like finances, work, or school). The individual with an obsession experiences anxiety and attempts to suppress such thoughts or impulses or "neutralize" them with another thought or action (that is, a compulsion). The person with an obsession is distressed by its presence; it is an *unwanted* intrusion into his thought life.

Common obsessions include:

- Repeated thoughts about contamination. This fear is the most common obsession.
- Repeated doubts (wondering whether you turned off the iron or hit someone while driving).
- A need to have things in a particular order, or a need to do a task "just right."
- Aggressive or horrific impulses (to hurt one's child or to shout an obscenity in church).
- Sexual imagery (such as a recurrent pornographic image).
- An irrational, persistent fear of developing a life-threatening illness.
- Hoarding (the inability to discard things such as newspapers and magazines).

Compulsions are "repetitive behaviors or mental acts, the goal of which is to prevent or reduce anxiety or distress."[3] The person does not carry out these behaviors or thought processes for pleasure. Rather, she feels driven to perform the compulsion to reduce the anxiety that accompanies an obsession. Someone with a contamination obsession might wash her hands thirty times a day. Someone with intrusive and unwanted aggressive impulses might count to twenty forward and backward for each aggressive thought. Compulsions are clearly excessive and are not connected in a realistic way with what they are designed to neutralize or prevent.

Common compulsions include:

- Repetitive behaviors (checking, washing, cleaning, requesting or demanding assurances, ordering and arranging, doing and undoing certain tasks in an exact sequence)
- Mental acts (counting, repeating words silently)
- Hoarding

The DSM description helps focus our attention on the experience of the sufferer and shapes the data-gathering questions that can help us determine the extent and severity of the counselee's struggle. At the same time, we must remember that a description does not explain *why* someone struggles with obsessive thoughts and compulsive behaviors. To answer that, we need a biblical view of human nature that provides a foundation for a biblical counseling approach.

What Causes OCD?

A biblical view of human beings affirms the "inner" and "outer" aspects to our design, which function together as a unity of spirit and body as we live before God and others. One term that Scripture uses to describe the inner aspect of a human being is the word "heart."[4] In both the Old and New Testaments, the heart refers to the basic inner orientation of the person, who either lives in covenant obedience or disobedience before God. The term "heart" expresses the reality that, at our core, we are all worshipers of *something*, either of the Creator (in obedience) or of created things (in disobedience), as seen in Romans 1.

God has designed us to express the worship of our hearts through our bodies. Our thoughts, our emotions, and our behaviors are all expressed through our body, though they all originate in the heart and express our worship.[5] Our bodies do not have the "final say" in whether our thoughts, emotions, and actions honor or dishonor God, but the Scriptures recognize the profound impact that our bodily weaknesses and limitations can have on us. Obedience may indeed be more difficult in the midst of bodily weakness and we must take this into account in our counseling approach.[6]

In bringing wise counsel to those who struggle with OCD, we want to distinguish between potential bodily stressors and the active responses of the heart. Most of us tend to overemphasize one or the other, leading to unbalanced counsel that either addresses heart issues of faith, obedience, and disobedience exclusively or bodily issues exclusively. To avoid these extremes we must ask, "What are the potential brain-based influences and pressures and what are the potential heart (worship) issues in someone struggling with OCD?"[7]

Potential Brain-Based Influences

Familial and genetic studies of OCD have shown a higher incidence rate among identical twins than fraternal twins, suggesting that some predisposition to obsessional behavior might be inherited.[8] While no definite conclusions can be drawn, it should at least make us aware that a person *may* be born with certain physical predispositions to struggle in this way.

In addition, the worldwide influenza epidemic of the early 1900s provided some of the first evidence that obsessive-compulsive symptoms can be associated with specific regions of the brain. Some patients developed not only Parkinson's-like symptoms (muscle tremors, slowed movement), but psychiatric symptoms, including obsessive-compulsive behaviors. Autopsies showed damage in the basal ganglia, a set of structures deep within the brain.[9] OCD has also been observed following head trauma.

One of the more compelling reasons to grapple with the biological factors that may influence the development of OCD is the sudden onset of OCD behaviors in children who have had strep throat. Antibiotics not only resolve the strep throat but usually terminate the OCD behaviors as well.

These examples suggest that some types of OCD may be more biologically based. We must take that into consideration, just as we would acknowledge that certain medical conditions can precipitate depression, such as a low-functioning thyroid.

In addition, "live action" brain scans such as PET scans or functional MRIs show an overactivity in the basal ganglia and frontal regions in the brain of a person struggling with OCD. This hyperactivity decreases with treatment.[10]

Many scientists believe that the neurotransmitter serotonin is involved in OCD because of the effectiveness of medications like Zoloft for OCD symptoms.[11] While altered neurochemicals (serotonin and others) may indeed be part of the "bodily pressure" involved in OCD, there is no current way to prove this as "the ultimate cause." Because there is a unity of the heart and body, we know that there will always be—at the very least—a biological *correlation:* a visible, measurable (more or less) connection between the spirit and the body. The brain scans reveal this correlation, but they cannot confirm that changes in the brain *cause* the obsessive thinking and ritualistic compulsions. Pre-existing, altered neurochemicals and brain circuitry *might* pressure us to respond in certain ways, but isn't it equally possible that the reverse is true—that the state of our hearts—our thoughts and beliefs about God, ourselves, and the world around us—may affect the levels of neurochemicals in our brains?[12]

Potential Heart Issues

While it is important to consider the potential bodily influences in this struggle, it is absolutely critical to address the dynamics of the heart that could lead to the experience of OCD. Did you ever wonder why someone struggles with anxiety in a more general way while someone else might struggle with OCD? Why is the first person's anxiety "reality-based" (worries about losing a job, caring for an elderly parent, etc.) and why is the second person's anxiety less "reality-based" (worries that I might throw my infant son through the window)? And why does the second person respond to this anxiety with ritualistic, compulsive behavior?

In part, the answer to that question can be traced to the motivations of the human heart. We are purposeful creatures made in the image of God, not merely robots responding to neurochemical events in our brains. We want, we desire, we hope, we yearn, we fear. Therefore, we must examine the spiritual dynamic behind OCD to offer hope for lasting change. As helpful as it is to ease the physical symptoms, the ultimate goal is for a person to forsake the sinful inclinations of his or her heart, to embrace the transforming hope of the gospel, and to grow in tangible ways to love God and others.

What are some spiritual (heart) issues that may generate this struggle? Not every person will have all of the following, but this overview should help identify some of the major motivational themes in OCD.

One of the major themes is **the need for certainty.** The person feels unable to live with uncertainty, needs total assurance, and seeks exhaustive and certain knowledge. OCD has been described as "the doubting disease." People with OCD characteristically doubt what they see with their own eyes, so they attempt to control the environment (the checking ritual) to erase that doubt and be certain. Thus, the need for certainty is tied to **the demand for control or mastery.** Ironically, the attempt to control the universe "bites back." People are mastered by their struggle to gain certainty and control. For some, this standard of absolute certainty brings doubts about their salvation and even undermines their ability to speak. ("How do I know that what I just said was accurate and true? Better to keep silent than risk saying something that is not absolutely correct.") Another facet of this demand for certainty or control may be a perceived **need for order.**

Another common theme is the **expectation of perfection**—the desire to be or do things "just right," the fear of being wrong. The focus here is on a "works" orientation, the pressure to do everything right. This particular heart dynamic may be especially active in people who struggle with aggressive or horrific impulses. They cannot deal with the fact that this thought entered their minds. "How could I think such a thing? Could I really do it? It's outrageous to think I could do such a thing! But what if I did?" This hypersensitivity and the ensuing guilt and anxiety lead to a self-oriented, mad scramble to overcome and neutralize the thought by some compensatory thought or behavior (the compulsion). "I can make things right; I can pay for this sin by doing this ritual, etc." OCD has an "it's all up to me" mentality, but the performance (whether it be checking or ordering or whatever ritualistic behavior occurs) is never enough. There is always yet another hoop to jump through.

In a sense, the compulsions are tangible works, revealing the false belief that "If I just do this one thing, my conscience will be clear and my anxiety will leave." Somehow, it seems safer to live by a self-imposed ritual than to face the disturbing thought head-on.

The issue of perfectionism is closely tied to **guilt,** another common theme in OCD. When I speak of guilt, I am mainly referring to the obsessions that center on the fear of doing (or having done) something horribly bad. But is this real guilt for real sin or is it guilt arising from *potential* sin? In most cases, it is the latter, yet the experience of guilt is real and it moves the person into **self-atonement.**

In a sense, one aspect of OCD involves people trying to atone for their own (imagined) sins through their "neutralizing" compulsions, creating a cycle of self-righteousness and despair. The neutralizing effect of the completed compulsion lasts just a short while (the self-righteous phase). This is soon replaced by a renewed obsession and the anxiety and self-loathing (despair) that go with it. The compulsion ("sacrifice") atones for the obsession ("sin"). It is a cultic, ritualistic system that bypasses the once-for-all sacrifice of Christ, and thus offers no lasting hope.

A final dynamic often present in the heart of an OCD struggler is **fear of man.** "What will others think?" is the refrain in their minds. There can be endless ruminations in which conversations are replayed over and over again. Sometimes the fear of making a mistake in front of others (related to perfectionism) will lead to increasing tentativeness in making decisions, answering questions, or offering opinions. Once again, this ironically backfires, and the desire to "do right" in front of others leads to a self-focus that disregards others' needs and concerns.

In what follows, I will assume that there is an earnest attempt by the counselor to connect with the OCD struggler, to listen, to love, to seek to understand, to truly enter into the struggle. What follows is not a "cookbook" approach, but a framework for speaking the truth in love.

Identify and Address Heart Issues Biblically

First, remember that not all doubt is sin! It is certainly not sinful to merely ask, "Have I locked the door?" and to check if you have. The issue is more clearly a sinful struggle when the desire to be sure becomes a demanding tyrant that generates anxiety and disrupts the Godward and others-centered focus that the Scriptures would have for us.

Similarly, the fleeting experience of a graphic image or impulse may not be sin in and of itself. It may well be *temptation to sin*. How many of us have had fleeting, irrational thoughts, only to lay them aside without further reflection? What I do with such thoughts is what reveals my heart. Do I nurse and cherish them with pleasure? Do I respond, as in OCD, with displeasure, anxiety, fear, and dread, and engage in a ritualistic, cleansing routine? These more deeply rooted responses of the heart are the issue in OCD.

What follows is a list of heart (spiritual) issues that may be related to OCD. These categories are not exhaustive and there is much overlap among them. As you consider them, note, too, that some heart issues are more clearly associated with one particular kind of obsession or compulsion, so what is helpful for one person may be less relevant for another.

Need for Certainty

In one sense, the struggle with OCD raises some valid questions: What is my reason for being sure of *anything?* How *can* I trust my senses? How *can* I make a decision and then rest in it? What is the foundation for *any* judgment I make?

Part of the problem in OCD is the "self-contained" nature of the struggle. My internal logic and reason, even my actual sensory experience, seemingly cannot convince me that my emotion (anxiety) is irrational and therefore safely ignored. When I think this way, I do not understand that, ultimately, my reason for being certain about anything does not come from within me: it comes from the outside, from the triune God as he reveals himself in Scripture. Truth, assurance, and certainty have their foundation in a covenant-making, promise-keeping God. What's more, God's promises come clothed in the form of a person, the Redeemer, Jesus Christ. "For no matter how many promises God has made, they are 'Yes' in Christ." (2 Cor. 1:20).

This is much more than a cognitive battle; it's really a battle of trust. Do I *trust* that God has revealed enough to enable me to live with what might be called "faithful" or "functional" certainty (which is not the same as 100 percent exhaustive knowledge)? Or will I continue to insist that the foundation for my certainty lies in me, in *my* "seeing"?

This struggle with certainty is the problem behind assurance issues, particularly assurance of salvation. The solution is not to add up the evidence that "proves" that I am a Christian (to have faith in my anemic faith) but to gaze long and hard at the person and character of Christ, on whom my faith ultimately rests. In other words, it's not the *strength* of my faith that counts, but the One in whom I place my faith.

If my faith is directed toward Jesus, then I am able to act even if I still have some small measure of doubt. I don't need to be 100 percent certain to act in faith. Reliance upon Jesus helps conquer remaining doubt, just as it did for the father whose son Jesus healed (see Mark 9:14–32, especially 9:24).

It can help an OCD sufferer to realize that he lives with "functional certainty" in most areas of his life. I recently asked a counselee struggling with incapacitating doubt why he could come into my office and sit in the chair without a second thought. His response was, "I just knew the chair would hold me." In other words, he implicitly *trusted the character* of the chair without having to check its structure to be sure.

In a similar way, trust in the person, character, and work of God is what breaks the obsession-compulsion connection. In the midst of rising doubt and anxiety, I must relinquish the quest for certainty (fueled by the attitude that "seeing is believing"), and choose instead to trust God's oversight of my life. It will be hard at first to walk away from the compulsion to check "to be sure," but with each resistance based on the character and care of God, the drive for certainty is less. Similarly, if my doubt is reflected in an unwillingness to answer questions until I can come up with a 100 percent accurate and truthful answer, the solution is to speak out of love for the other person anyway, trusting God's Spirit to conform my thinking to his, and accepting the fact that I won't have perfect knowledge of myself in this life.

Demand for Control and Mastery

If the need for certainty and the inability to live with doubt underlie much obsessional thinking, it is the quest for control, primarily over rising anxiety, that manifests itself in compulsive behaviors. To control my anxiety, I seek to control or manipulate my environment: "If I bolt and rebolt the door three times, *then* I can be certain." But shrinking my world to a manageable area—checking the lock, cleaning the sink, reciting a ritualized prayer—does not control my fear for long. Mastery exists just for a moment. And just as trick birthday candles erupt in flame again and again, so the anxiety returns because the extinguishing power of God's real and loving care is not experienced in the moment. Freedom begins to come as the OCD sufferer gives up the need to control his anxiety and his world and casts himself upon the grace and providential care of God.

Psalm 139 is a helpful place to turn because it reminds us of God's complete knowledge of us and his detailed oversight of our lives. It reminds us of the "guardrails of God's providence."[13] Consider the following verses:

- "You know when I sit and when I rise; you perceive my thoughts from afar. You discern my going out and my lying down; you are familiar with all my ways. Before a word is on my tongue you know it completely, O LORD. You hem me in—behind and before; you have laid your hand upon me."(vv. 2–5)
- "If I rise on the wings of the dawn, if I settle on the far side of the sea, even there your hand will guide me, your right hand will hold me fast." (vv. 9–10)
- "All the days ordained for me were written in your book before one of them came to be." (v. 16)

How does the psalmist respond to this realization? "Such knowledge is too wonderful for me" (v. 6). "Your works are wonderful, I know that full well" (v. 14). "How precious to me are your thoughts, O God!" (v. 17). Although the psalmist recognizes the complexity of God's world and his oversight, he is content to leave that ultimate control in the hands of God. In fact, praise erupts! Ultimately I am safe in him. Safety is not found in my own reasoning process or ritual. I am called to live responsibly before God, but I don't have *ultimate* responsibility or oversight of my life. Other psalms that address this theme include Psalms 104, 121, 127, and 131.

Desire for a "Black and White" World

OCD sufferers want to live in a black and white (all or nothing) world. Exhaustive knowledge, complete control, and absolute certainty allow no room for ambiguity. Either I'm sure or I'm not; either I'm in control or I'm not; either I'm right or I'm not. Yet we live in a gray world: God reveals enough knowledge to live sanely before him, but he doesn't give us full access to his mind (see Job 38–41). God gives us the ability to choose freely and to act, but we cannot master all the details of our world. God gives us direction in his Word, but many issues are not clear-cut. This shows the importance of the biblical category of wisdom. It's "safer" to live in a black and white world, because it requires no trust! But trust and wisdom go hand in hand (as Job found out!).

Perfectionism, Guilt, and Self-atonement

Differentiate actual sin from potential sin. For people struggling with OCD, possibility equals reality. They react to the "what if" possibility as though they had actually committed the terrible act that came into their minds. On the one hand, someone with OCD may have an over-scrupulous conscience. On the other hand, because the volume of their conscience has been turned up so loud on *potential* sins (like yelling an obscenity during a sermon), their conscience becomes hardened to the ways in which they actually *do* transgress the law of God (like ignoring one's family in the midst of a complex counting ritual). At the very least, they are confusing the *temptation* to sin with actually *committing* the sin.[14] More seriously, when they think about potential sins, they miss the "more important matters of the law—justice, mercy and faithfulness" (Matt. 23:23–24).

"Cheer up, you're worse than you think." The fact of the matter is, apart from the sustaining grace of Christ, I am capable of atrocities far worse than any that have entered my mind. Why should I be so surprised by the content of a fleeting thought? Church planter and seminary professor Jack Miller coined the

phrase, "Cheer up, you're worse than you think," to undermine the self-righteousness of someone who continues to wallow in his sin—in our case, potential sin—and refuses to grab hold of the righteousness of Christ.

Lay hold of the remedy for real guilt from real sin. This ties the preceding two points together. Forgiveness is available for actual sins, not imagined ones. Christ didn't die for potential sinners; he died for actual sinners whose guilt could only be taken away by his atoning sacrifice. And his sacrifice is enough! His work is not the temporary neutralization of potential evil; it is a once-for-all, permanent destruction of the worst evil imaginable. This is why the entire book of Hebrews (particularly chapters 8–10) can be immensely helpful for the OCD struggler. As you gaze at the character and work of Jesus Christ—his finished work on the cross, his ongoing intercession for his people, etc.—the need to self-atone or establish a self-righteousness will diminish.

Self-cleansing, either for the true guilt of real sin or the "false" guilt[15] of imagined sins (in OCD) is never enough. All your penance, all your regrets, all your anxieties, all your sacrifices and compensatory duties are not enough. Only the blood of Christ is enough.

And it is that very sacrifice that can embolden you to step into the light to forsake the real sin: the self-absorption in which an OCD sufferer is caught. Jesus has kept all the important standards. He has done everything that needs to be done and he has done it right. Any additional standard we impose saps the vitality from that restful reality. Let that joyful reality break the need to act out a compulsion and you will find that the guilty grip of your obsession will loosen.

Live as a son or daughter and not as an orphan. Someone struggling with OCD often views God as a harsh taskmaster, a capricious deity with oppressive demands. A person with OCD often lives under a film of displeasure. If you are a Christian, your identity is not that of an orphan ("It's all up to me; I can't trust anyone; I must control my life and destiny"). It is that of a son or daughter on whom the Father's favor rests. That brings freedom from the tyranny of performance and perfectionism.

Identify and Address Potential Body Issues

If a normal child suddenly develops obsessive-compulsive behaviors in conjunction with a sore throat, it would be wise to seek medical help immediately. If a streptococcal infection is present, antibiotics will cure the infection and should also decrease or end the OCD behaviors.

But what about the vast majority of OCD cases, where the onset of the struggle is insidious and progressive? How much attention should we pay to the potential bodily influences? Remember that the content of the obsession (and *perhaps* even its frequency) may not be sin in and of itself, but simply a bodily stressor.[16]

While affirming that the body and brain are ultimately not the "cause" of sin, we should not underestimate the overwhelming tyranny that these bombarding thoughts can exert on these sufferers. At the same time, we can also affirm that as the OCD struggler addresses the heart issues involved, the symptoms (the frequency and severity of the obsessions and compulsions) should decrease.

In biologically oriented psychiatry, to cure the symptom *is* to cure the problem. Obsessive-compulsive thoughts and behaviors are thought to be caused by a disordered brain, so if you treat the symptoms with medication *or* with cognitive-behavioral therapy (which both work on the brain, directly and indirectly, respectively), you have attacked the underlying disorder. Both approaches may bring a measure of symptom relief, sometimes substantial. But our ultimate goal as biblical counselors is more than symptom relief. We believe that as the counselee grapples, applies, and is transformed by biblical truth at the heart level, his "disordered" brain patterns *will also* change and symptom relief will occur. How could it be otherwise, given the way God made us?

Still, there may be a time and place for targeting the symptoms themselves, particularly if the person's struggle is so severe that he cannot benefit from counseling. The use of medication is a wisdom issue and must be individualized for each counselee. There are biblical guidelines for making such a decision, but there is no "one size fits all" approach.[17] We must beware of black and white thinking that would uphold *either* the relief of suffering (physical or mental) *or* the benefit of suffering as the more biblical approach. The Bible speaks positively about *both* the relief of suffering and the benefits of enduring it. If medication is used, we must remember that it is relieving symptoms, nothing more. That approach *may* be wise for certain individuals with severe symptoms, but we must never lose sight of the heart dynamics invariably present with OCD.

Although it is helpful, even necessary, to differentiate between spiritual issues and bodily weakness to counsel wisely, this will not always be easy. A certain sense of mystery remains as we seek to do this task, so we must set about this ministry with humility. At the end of the day, we must ask, have we approached the person struggling with OCD as both a sufferer and a sinner, speaking and incarnating the truth and hope of the gospel in love?

Notes

1   The description that follows is based on the American Psychiatric Association [hereafter APA], *Diagnostic and Statistical Manual of Mental Disorders* (Washington, D.C.: American Psychiatric Association, 2000), 4th ed., text revision, 456–63. While I disagree with the unspoken premise that all the problems described in the DSM have a purely biological cause, the detailed *descriptions* in the DSM can help biblical counselors understand the scope and severity of the struggle, and aid communication with others seeking to help the counselee.

2   APA, 457.

3   Ibid.

4   See Deut. 6:5; Josh. 22:5; 1 Sam. 13:14; 16:7; 1 Chron. 28:9; Ps. 14:1 (and many other psalms); Prov. 4:23; 27:19; Jer. 24:7; Matt. 5:8; 6:21. The Bible also uses other terms to capture this inner aspect of human beings, including spirit, soul, mind, will, conscience, hidden self, and inner nature (see Ezek. 11:19; Matt. 10:28; John 7:17; Rom. 2:15; 2 Cor. 4:16; Col. 1:21; Heb. 8:10; 1 Peter 3:4).

5   See Gen. 6:5; Deut. 8:5; Prov. 2:10; Eph. 1:18; 4:18; Heb. 4:12 (thoughts); Gen. 6:6; Lev. 19:17; Prov. 13:12; 14:13; 24:17 (emotions); Ex. 25:2; Luke 6:45; Eph. 6:6 (actions).

6   Here's a simple example: if I tend to get angry and irritable after several poor nights of sleep, I need to do more than repent of the heart-based roots of my anger (which I should do). I *also* need to get some sleep! I'm responsible for my actions, sleepy or not,

but my approach includes addressing the bodily weakness with the physical "treatment" of sleep.

7 Because of space considerations, I will not discuss interpersonal influences (the role of family upbringing) or societal-cultural influences, both of which may impact OCD and are worth exploring to make our approach as biblically robust as possible.

8 American Psychiatric Association, *The American Psychiatric Textbook of Psychiatry*, 3rd ed. (Washington, D.C.: American Psychiatric Press), 603.

9 The basal ganglia regulate several phenomena including movement, cognition, and emotion.

10 Interestingly, the changes occur whether treatment is with medication or counseling.

11 Zoloft is part of a family of medications called "selective serotonin reuptake inhibitors" (SSRIs), which are thought to affect the levels of serotonin in different regions of the brain.

12 Although secular models assume that the primary cause is biological, one of the most successful secular treatments for OCD (a cognitive-behavioral model) is based on the reverse assumption—that I can change the pattern of my brain chemistries by first changing my thinking.

13 I am indebted to Jim Petty for coining this phrase in his book, *Step by Step* (Phillipsburg, N.J.: P&R, 1999), 76.

14 In fact, you could argue that the horrific and aggressive impulses are not true temptations in the biblical sense of the word. While it is true that they are thoughts that could only occur in a fallen world, they don't fit the description offered in James 1:13–15.

The person struggling with OCD is *not* enticed by the horrific impulse; he is repulsed. The *true temptation* is, "Will I trust the sufficiency of Christ's sacrifice for me or will I try to atone for my own actions (wrongly perceived as sin)?"

15 By "false guilt" I don't mean that the person does not have a real experience of guilt. I mean that the guilt they feel about the *content* of the obsession has no basis in reality.

16 However, I believe that the more one attempts to deal with the anxiety induced by the obsession in an unbiblical way, the more intrusive and persistent the obsession may become. In that situation, the frequency of the obsession becomes part of the heart dynamic.

17 For a concise discussion of the issues involved in medication, see Edward T. Welch, *Blame It on the Brain?* (Phillipsburg, N.J.: P&R, 1998), 108–09. Potential relief of symptoms with medication (which is less reliable for OCD than for some other psychiatric problems), must be balanced with potential negative effects of being on medication.

Michael R. Emlet *is a counselor and faculty member at the Christian Counseling & Educational Foundation in Glenside, Pennsylvania.*

RCL Ministry Booklets

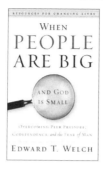

"Ed Welch is a good physician of the soul. This book is enlightening, convicting, and encouraging. I highly recommend it."

—JERRY BRIDGES

". . . refreshingly biblical. . . . brimming with helpful, readable, practical insight."

—JOHN MACARTHUR

"Readable and refreshing. . . . goes to the heart of an issue immobilizing the church. Exposes and repudiates the trivia of therapeutic theology with wisdom and compassion."

—SUSAN HUNT

COUNSELING RESOURCES

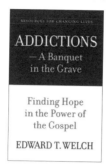

"Biblically sound, practical, filled with Christ-like compassion. . . . This much-needed book offers real hope and the promise of victory in Jesus to those struggling with addiction."

—ROBERT A. EMBERGER, Whosoever Gospel Mission

"This is vital reading for church leaders, and for friends and family desiring to help those struggling with addictions."

—JOHN FREEMAN, HARVEST USA